The Journey

Pathway to Success

volume 2

Georgiana Smith

ISBN: 979-8-35097-208-5

DEDICATION

I dedicate this book to my loving husband Richard who has helped me and continues to help on this journey. Although everyone's journey begins at birth, meeting a person who can take the journey with you, guide you and even sail the heavy storms is a blessing. I appreciate being on this journey with him and look forward to continuing the journey with him by my side until the end of our time. He is truly my better half and, the true definition of God sent. Our hopes are that we create a path that leads our children down a successful journey.

TABLE OF CONTENTS

THE JOURNEY

Life is a journey, and the journey of life is indeed a beautiful one. We are pilgrims and sojourners in this world, but our journey through life isn't without ups and downs. If I may ask; how has been your journey here on earth?

If you examine the word "Journey" most definitions will read "an act of traveling from one place to another. "My definition is similar but a little more explicit based on my life and my journey. Journey to me is traveling through life's unknown obstacles, tasks, titles, pain, suffering, good times, extraordinary moments, unknown moments, praying for the best but preparing for the worse, having great times, but having to deal with tough times, surviving obstacles, happy yet sometimes sad, wanting to be loved but don't mind being disliked.

I can go on and on about my definition of "my Journey" The true definition doesn't express the things we encounter as we travel from one place to the other. It just states traveling from one place to another and nothing in between. But the between in the journey is the essence of it. What we become along the way is what defines the purpose of our journey.

I am happy to be on this continued journey and although we make plans, a major part of life's journey is the unknown challenges that come up along the way to take you off course. How you continue is all up to you. Your journey is not the same as mine yet, at certain points we will experience uncertainties, doubts, fears and worries. These are common realities that we all share as we forge ahead through life. The beauty of life is that we can always share from the experiences of others and that is why I believe in baring my mind out so you can see that you are not alone, and the world is waiting for you to go all out and discover every part of it just as you learn to find yourself.

Throughout my life's journey, I have become a mother, a wife, a friend, a student, a teacher and a business owner. Etc. I have evolved to see the transience of life and the endless possibilities that are open to me.

I have had the opportunity to travel throughout my life to my parent's country Panama, my husband's country numerous times Jamaica and many other states within the U.S., however going to Africa in 2024 was a journey I took through Egypt, Ghana and Morocco. Africa was a life-changing experience, something I will never forget. The experience was spiritual, emotional, mental and educational an experience a major part of my continued JOURNEY.

Experiencing different languages, different foods, different lifestyles, different religions, and different cultures was truly an experience. There were so many surreal moments throughout this journey that brought me to tears. Tears of joy, tears, of pain, tears of disbelief. The joy was being blessed for the experience, the pain was the past hurt allowing me to have the opportunity to experience those moments, tears of disbelief knowing that my journey has brought me to a place I only heard about in history.

Africa taught me that my journey is not only meant to be in one place, but also for me to continue around the world exploring and learning more about myself and how I can help others while my journey continues. This is indeed a pointer to how life can be transformative and dynamic. I have always wondered what really defines us as individuals. Is it what we are or what we become?

Most people do not get to enjoy their journey through life because they are crippled with the fear of what the future will bring. Often, we do not know better and it's certainly not our fault. There are certain realities that we must come to terms with if we are going to get a chance at making the most of our journey. And as we grapple with them, we see parts of ourselves being revealed to us. My intention is to share with you, certain truths that I have been able to glean from life. Do I have all the answers? Certainly not but as the journey continues, I will continue to discover and overcome hurdles as I enhance my path with my experience and knowledge along the way. As it is often said you either get better or bitter.

CHAPTER ONE

LESSONS ALONG THE WAY

Life itself can be a lesson learned based on the different events that occur in the world that affect our everyday operation, things we cannot control. One of the things I think that affected everyone's journey was COVID. Everyone had to adapt to a different way of living. Through the fears of watching hundreds die, not knowing would the world survive this, the journeys of life continued, the sun still rose, the nights still came, and we had to learn to deal with it. I learned that we cannot control the things that may come along the journey, however we can adapt, make changes, or continue to plan for the best. During Covid I began to adapt and continue to plan for the best, because if this was going to be a new norm there was not much I could have done to stop it aside from learn how to live with it and try and make the appropriate adjustments to continue my journey.

I have learned that people including family come and go, however they will always be a part of your journey because you have encountered them in some shape or form. I have learned that you can't choose your family, and you sometimes can't choose the people you encounter on your journey. You can control your peace by accepting, and not accepting, certain elements that may be produced in relationships. Relationships cover all types, business, family, social, friends, non-friends etc. People make the world go round is a saying we all have heard, and people are a part of everyone's journey.

I have learned that what makes a Boss is not a title it's the work you put into the business or whatever you oversee. I have learned that you can't take things for face value, and when someone shows you who they are the first time BELIEVE IT!!!!!

They say money changes people. I have witnessed how money changed the people around me. Of course you try to remain the same, but regardless things will change for you. You will begin to do things you have never done, buy the things you always wanted, go places you never been. I just try to remember where I came from and that keeps me grounded.

My husband plays a major part in keeping me grounded and humble. He still mows the lawn, builds things inside and outside of the house. His motto is "I am not paying anyone when I can do it myself". One of my hardest lessons learned as a CEO is not looking further into information that was provided to me that literally cost me $604,000 dollars. Yes $604,000 dollars let me further explain. I was provided information that was not accurate under the state laws of Virginia, becoming a business owner in the field of Individuals with Intellectual and Development Disabilities my husband and I knew how to work with Individuals and how to run the operation. We maintained all standards and regulations that were needed to ensure services were provided, we paid someone who handled some business aspects and advised us wrongly. Even though it would be easy for us to place all blame on this professional person, we could have even gone to the extent to file a legal complaint and grievance, but we were guilty of not educating ourselves, especially as the company began to grow. The lesson was costly and caused a lot of emotional stress. If I were to say it was only the money, I would not be honest. It was the backlash of people assuming we were not legit, and that it was intentional. Even though we paid all the money back upon request the lesson learned is educate yourself.

Trust is a main factor for most people but let's be honest we all are introduced to the better side of a person, the better side of a business, a better side of things in general. No one meets a person and immediate tells them all their flaws, no one looking for a job discloses the things they will not do if they really want the job, no one tells you all the bad things first. These things are very unlikely to happen at the beginning of any introduction. Therefore, when the truth comes out trust goes down and another side of you is revealed. Most times we meet the representative of a person first. Who wants to tell someone their flaws first. I have learned to trust yourself and how you handle the information provided to you. I will say through my journey, time will always tell and if it doesn't it wasn't meant for me to know. I refuse to live my life wondering if someone is being honest to me. I expect honesty of course who doesn't, but what we expect and what happens are mostly two different things throughout the journey of life.

Learning that everything that glitters is not gold, and anything worth having is worth working for. I remember hearing these sayings and wondering what they were talking about. As I began to grow and understand the journey I was on. It all began to make sense. Everything I wanted looked so good when it wasn't mine but when it became mine it did not look so good anymore, and once I realized I had to maintain it as well as have it.

I wanted a husband to love me unconditionally and I got that, but I didn't realize I had to put down some of my old ways to get unconditional love. I wanted a nice car, a nice house, bags, shoes, you know what they call finer things of life. Material things are not the most important aspect of my life, but I still wanted them. I quickly learned that having it and keeping it took work and not just the work to buy it, it also took work to maintain it. Too many people want to live a certain lifestyle but don't want to work to get it or endure the things someone else had to get it.

Whatever we desire to become will never come on a platter. There are no shortcuts to becoming what you want and anyone who tries to cut corners soon will find around the corner is a long road called life depending on your journey. We must be willing to understand that there are certain things about life that we must learn before we can grow into the next phase of what life has in store for us.

Let's use the analogy of formal education. For every subject that is being taught, there is always an examination to be given to ascertain the knowledge acquired by the student. Life examines us as well with trials and tribulations. We are taught as children don't touch the stove its hot, don't talk to strangers, look both ways before crossing. How many of these things did we do anyway and when it happened, we were upset. Even though we were told not to do it.

It is always easy to look at someone else's life and analyze what they are doing right and wrong. But take a good look at your life and you will understand there are lots of lessons that we skip every day because we are not paying attention.

Life is a lesson to those who are students of experience. It is often said we are spiritual beings having a human experience. Life has to be clearly defined for it to be fully grasped. How you see life defines what you learn. If you see life as someone who is just passing by then you will always learn to make temporary decisions and never commit yourself to anything worthwhile.

If you see yourself as someone who has a part to play in existence, you will soon learn that your role in the world is not defined by the perception of others.

If you are someone who seeks validation from people you will soon learn that when the praises turn to criticisms, you will lose yourself and your ambitions all because you have not learnt to see the world through your own eyes.

Most times, we fail to face the reality of what is in front of us and try to find an easy way out. Once we learn that we cannot change our reality and try to navigate through it we may just be able to prepare for life challenges and face them head on.

What do you do when you have learned a lesson that took you through a hard time? Do you make wine with the crushed grapes or do you stay mad with the assumption the grapes will become uncrushed. We must be open and willing to see that we are students of life. Life is not meant to be lived on autopilot. It's one of the reasons we keep repeating certain cycles and we wonder why we are not living to the fullness of our potential. Without lessons we cannot grow. And without growth our journey becomes a tedious affair. If life is a journey as we have established, then it means at every stop there's a lesson that is meant to instill in us a certain kind of mindset. It either builds us up or breaks us down. Something will happen. What we learn can make or break us. How we respond to the lessons learnt determines what we believe about ourselves.

I have seen people give up on certain pursuits just because they believed the situations turned out to be unfavorable. A devastating heartbreak can make a person shut out their heart to love. What this person fails to have realized is that it is a lesson in discernment. It is a lesson in hopeless sentimental attachments. That's the point. But we would rather shut our heart out and choose not to fall in love again, not understanding for someone to take care of your heart your heart has had to be broken before.

I have learnt that life is a series of chapters and the story you are currently living in is not the end of your chapter. I may not matter what you think right now what matters is your ability to see the finished line.

Most people try to run life as a sprint. And you would not have to blame them much seeing that we currently live in an age where people are expected to seem like they have it all figured out. We have seen a high level of comparison on social media. The desire to feel like we are there with others making the most of our lives. This has led many down the trail of depression and frustration and they have begun to feel like their loves do not matter. They have begun to see themselves as people without a sense of worth, because they are trying to live their lives based on others.

Social media was meant to reconnect to my understanding, share life stories, everyone has changed it including myself. Social media has become a way to debate, express feelings, show what you have, show what you don't have. It has put many in a place of trying to fit in forgetting who they are or really want to be. I have learnt that life comes in phases and people are in seasons. There are certain experiences that are necessary so you can have a story to tell.

Everyone loves a good ending, but few people want to endure what transpires at the beginning and the middle of the story. I have learnt that when you are going through life take it one day at a time so you can keep your sanity. Stop trying to go ahead with your plans. Yes, we should plan for the future, however, try conquering a day first. I have learnt that the worst fears are what we create when we are desperate to understand life in its totality. Life is to be lived and experienced. It is not for you to know all the answers. You learn answers on the way and utilize them along the journey with new obstacles. I have learnt that no one knows all the answers. That should give you some level of comfort in knowing that you are not alone when you struggle with cluelessness.

I have learnt that it is always good to start with what you have wherever you are. I have learnt that the problems we struggle with most of the times are because of our desire to control everything. You simply cannot control every outcome in life, but you can control how you respond to it.

When Covid took the world by storm, no one was expecting it. But a lot of people soon learnt that life could take a turn at any time and not just for one person but for the world. I believe Covid changed the world and taught everyone how to navigate a different way. If you made it through that drastic deadly change you have learned a life lesson.

Humans have survived several centuries and decades and one thing we seem to all agree upon is that times have changed. You will hear songs, see different clothes, and think life has changed. How is it that life has changed but some of us can't or don't want to. How are we growing and learning through the same eyes in a different time. We have witnessed plagues across the ages. We have seen wars of devastating consequences. We have witnessed the demise of loved ones across generational lines. We have seen the rich become poor and the poor become rich. We have seen miscreants become kings and kings become nothing. We have seen kingdoms rise and fall and small nations become mighty. And in all these experiences historians have woven several stories around them to make us see that there are always lessons to learn from the experiences of others.

In most cases we try to put experiences into practice. We try to organize and define our lives with what we have gleaned from the history of the past. But sooner or later at certain points of our lives we see that while these experiences may be similar the peculiarities and the circumstances around them are quite different and we may need a different approach to things. We often forget that our ideologies across time are different. This is why you see people often say experience is the best teacher. That may be correct but I believe you are what you make of your experience

I have learnt that life will test your beliefs. It will test all that you claim to know in situations that you can never really control. I have learnt that the first and last person to determine your success and failure is you. You have the leading role of your destiny, and you must always make sure that you take responsibility for your actions rather than outsource them to someone else.

I have learnt that love demands sacrifice. A lot of times we want a future we are seldom eager to labor for. We love people without putting in the effort to watch the relationship blossom. I have learnt that what you give to life comes back to you. I have learnt that you should never really judge anyone until you have experienced the kind of life they have lived. I have learnt that forgiveness is relevant to my wellbeing. That when we hold on to grudges and wrongs, we end up hurting our bodies and souls.

I have learnt that you need like minds to be able to move far. It's okay to move alone, but you need people who will strengthen you when the going gets tough. Life is not a sprint if you look at it that way you will exhaust yourself before you get to the finished line. You want to enjoy the race and the finish.

There will always be lessons to learn from all our endeavors. Pay attention to all your lessons, even the worse ones. Take something from each lesson and build yourself to be stronger. Do not although the lesson learned to go in vain. Lessons learned will make you the better you.

CHAPTER TWO

CHALLENGES

Who wants to be challenged? I think that depends on the challenge. We would rather want a life of ease and comfort where we can determine what happens and filter out the bad days and moments. Our bodies are always sending us signals of flight or fight when faced with unfamiliar situations that threaten that sense of the norm. That shows us that we are built for challenges. Because we are challenged daily with our kids, our spouses, friends, family, jobs, the list goes on and on and normally begins with the closet people to us. Responses in us is a way to point us toward a solution. There would be no victory if we have not learnt battle. No success without the capacity for failure. No glory without the availability of pain. Challenges are a reality of human experience.

One of the ways in which we face challenges is in our expectations. Often, we have a certain perspective of the kind of life we want and what we want from others and when those things do not materialize, we suddenly feel a sense of fear like we have been left exposed and vulnerable. Expectations is a good thing because it sets the tone of what we demand from ourselves and others, but it is also important to note that you cannot always see the end of your expectations, you only have an idea of what to expect not what will happen. You can plan and plot towards the way you want things to go but you cannot ascertain what will happen at every step of the way.

My challenges along this journey began in my early years as discussed in my first book Pathway to Success Trauma to Triumph. My challenges play a major part of my journey. Coming from a divorce home was a challenge for me in my marriage. My mother raising me alone most times showed me strength of a woman without a man, therefore when I got married the first few years that was how I operated. That was a challenge that could of ruined my marriage. I had to learn that my marriage was not like the one my mother had that failed, mines had a strong man who didn't have to walk around saying I am the man his presence, his way of doing things, and ensuring his family was taken care of showed he was the man.

Being a teenage mom was a challenge, but more so when I began to have other children. I had to learn I was raising children and not growing up with them. I had to adjust to new times and life's changes. My challenge was changing with time and raising my kids the way I wanted and not how I was raised.

Relationships challenged me. I went through years of relationships with expectations. When I realized you can still love someone without being close to them my life changed for the better. One of my biggest challenges in relationships is when life changes you have to change with it you cannot remain the same which means some of the things you used to do you may not be able to do any more. My mind changed and that led me to doing different things, wanting more, which meant some of the old things had to be out down, I did think that meant people, but I learned quickly it did. It is challenging to walk away or be pushed away from relationships you have been around for some time. I just believe some people last through many seasons and some people don't.

Transitioning though is a challenge it can be very difficult to walk into new experiences. We are all creatures of habit moat times. New is wanted but can be scary when you're unsure. Starting a business was very challenging, so much so that even when my husband and I started our business we both were afraid of leaving our old jobs. We would soon be responsible for paying others and ensuring we were paid and able to support our family through our own company. This was a challenge we still face five years later with over fifty employees three programs.

Health is always a big challenge. When you get sick the first thought is am I going to be ok. There is a story behind every sickness and google doesn't make it better. We are challenged by life everyday things, yet we fail to be able to conquer them when they are first presented. It is called the unknown. Let's be honest we cannot predict every outcome, obstacle, or force that comes behind each challenge.

Another major part of my journey that is really challenging is the aging of my parents. It is hard to come to terms with watching them decline and not being able to do much about the inevitable. Trying to be a wife, mother etc., can be hard but being a caretaker, the decision maker, is challenging when your parents begin to age. My mom battled cancer back in 2019 at the age of 73; I cared for her while living in Virginia and she lived in New York. I traveled back and forth until she was cancer free.

My dad developed Parkinson's and has declined progressively. Watching him has been the hardest thing of my life and although he wasn't the greatest father he was the best daddy. I am now in a place where I am grieving the parents I once knew while being a care giver making difficult decisions regarding their level of care. This is a challenge I rather have not take but I had no choice. Being my dad's only child and the one my mom depends on the most is very difficult.

My challenges and disappointments are a major part of my continued journey. I now look forward to a challenge because I know it places me one step a ahead each time I conquer a challenge and once I am moving forward I am using the challenge for my best interest.

You may think you have a blueprint on the reality of your situation and create a template on the most crucial aspect of that situation. For example, if you want to own a business. Your expectation is that you make profit. Which is fair enough, but you must also realize that there is more to running a business. You also need to understudy the business before seeking funds. Blind expectations can cripple your mind and spirit. This is called a challenge. You are not just plunging in head on without weighing the pros and cons.

As for your expectations of individuals, learn not to place people on pedestals. Be realistic enough to know that man has a limited capacity to do all that is required to meet all our expectations. They can only give to the best of their capacities. The sooner you realize this, the better you become at owning yourself and the outcome of some of your challenges.

There are challenges that come with disappointments. This is one challenge that tends to limit people from fulfilling all there is to their destiny. It feels like all that we have built has been destroyed and there is no way out of it. Why have we been treated unfairly? Why have we been abandoned after placing all our hopes on them? Why did we get shortchanged over that deal? How can we not get that thing we have so much labored for? When we ask these questions repeatedly it often turns out that we have reshaped our reality of things. We can easily define our lives from the prism of disappointments. We tell ourselves. I will not love again. Maybe that business isn't for me. Maybe I can't have a good family because my parents failed.

We begin to see ourselves through disappointment as it begins to feel like that is a reality. We fail to see that whatever it is that is happening in that moment is just temporary. Disappointments/ challenges are a limitation to the extent to which we allow them to define us. Yes, you read that right. Lots of people have gone on to build wonderful lives through disappointments and challenges.

Imagine Thomas Edison giving up on making the light bulb after nine hundred disappointments. He would not have been able to see the end of the light bulb's success.

When we magnify disappointments/ challenges we have placed ourselves in a situation where solutions or alternatives are far from reach.

There are certain areas of our lives that require a level of disappointment and challenge to wake us up from our slumber. In fact, certain kinds of disappointments and challenges are a blessing in disguise because we may never know what we could achieve if we do not let go of what we think we have acquired.

Sometimes we hold on so tight to life not knowing that there are certain things that are in store for us. Always see an opportunity in a challenge to get something better.

The challenge of disconnections from environments or people we have come to build a life with can have a debilitating effect on our experience. We are social creatures, and it is only natural that we find a sense of belonging within a community. When we disconnect from the familiar, we struggle with loneliness and fear. We begin to ask ourselves if it is possible to find any meaning or belonging to anyone else. But the world is not confined to our limited space. The world is a vast expanse of possibilities that gives us access to different places and people. Disconnections are not death sentences, rather they are lessons on the seasonal nature of life. We often fail to realize that most connections are not really leading us anywhere.

We place sentimental attachments to certain connections, and it hinders us from seeing what we can possibly become when we launch out of the familiar. There are certain connections that limit our growth, and it takes a kind of fortitude to realize that disconnecting from such situations and environments is only for our own good. What drives our dissatisfaction with disconnection most times is the uncertainty of what lies ahead. It is not a bad thing to rue a lost connection, but it is dangerous to put ourselves in a box thinking that we have lost ourselves when things do not go as planned.

The future is waiting to embrace you if you are willing to let go of the past. We are worthy of meaningful relationships. We deserve to be seen and heard. The earlier you bring yourself out of the box you have placed yourself in the better for your sanity. It's okay to feel overwhelmed over the disconnection but what you should not do is hinder yourself of becoming all that you can become. Take the challenge.

People fear moving ahead. It's called the unknown. They have grown up all their lives in one place and have become acquainted with it. And this becomes the only life they know. What they fail to realize in most cases is familiarity hinders growth. There is so much you can become if only you can set your mind to letting go of the familiar. Take the challenge! Do not be afraid of forging a new path because you do not know what can be birth that will change your life. Take the challenge.

Disconnections can only be a challenge when you allow yourself to be walled in with the comfort zone of the familiar. Most stages in life it is expected that we grow and most growth comes with leaving behind what is familiar while taking a new path that is being laid out before us. In the journey of life, you will always have reasons to make new discoveries. And as you move through it, you eventually realize that those things you held so much as your life were nothing compared to where you are currently.

The greatest challenge of grief is acceptance. Accepting that the person we are grieving over can never come back or the things we may grieve over may never be the same. Forgetting is a word used often without value. Do we ever forget hurt, pain, anguish or do we put it aside until we are at our lowest point or challenged with the unknown and remember it all to cause more pain. It hurts to always remember that you have lost a part of you that will never come back. A part of you that has defined your existence.

The thing about grief is that it doesn't give us a warning when it comes and even in those moments when we are expectant of someone's imminent demise, maybe from a protracted illness or a fatal diagnosis, there's always a sense of hope that lingers at the fringes, baiting us into thinking that we could still salvage the situation, till eventually we are smitten with the reality of the loss. My therapist gave me the best concept which was *"**You never get over the lost, You just learn how to live with the lost.**"*

We ask questions, we seek answers on how to move on, we bury ourselves in past memories, and we find ourselves wondering how to move on. The truth is, we can do little to control when grief hits us. Human existence can be fragile, and we are all on temporary timelines.

The first thing is to acknowledge that life is temporary. This would make us live meaningful lives and value moments we spend with people so when we relate with people around us, we do so from a place of appreciation for what the future may bring. And when the inevitable happens we can tell ourselves that we were able to make the most of our relationships with them.

Another thing to note about grief is that it opens you up to the urgency of what you are supposed to do rather than waiting for things to happen. You want to get that job? Go ahead and chase the dream now. You love someone? Tell them. We must always be willing to see life through the prism of its finitude. Every time we are faced with grief, we should also seek out ways to express ourselves. If you can't talk to someone, you could have a journal. Isolation only compounds grief. And while people grieve differently, there is always a sense that when we allow ourselves to be strengthened by others it becomes less bearable.

Every person will lose someone in their lifetime, it's something we cannot avoid. But what happens when we lose the people who are close to us can influence how we see the world. And we are to aspire towards optimism, and it also means that we find those who have gone through the same process we currently face and draw from their knowledge. We can only heal as much as we allow ourselves to.

When grief comes knocking, know that the weight of the pain will ease up with time. You may never be able to get over it in totality, but you can take a richer perspective about life which makes you appreciate different areas of your life again.

Through challenges we can learn parts of ourselves that we did not know we could even reach or exist. Through challenges we conquer our fears and those things we thought were impossible end up becoming just a figment of our imagination.

CHAPTER THREE

EMBRACING THE UNKNOWN

Why do babies cry when they are born? They are simply in a world of the unknown. For nine months they have been cocooned in their mothers' belly and it has given them everything they ever wanted and now they find themselves in the open, lights and different hands poking and prodding. Feeling what we call hunger, being wet and feeling icky. And then it dawns on them, that the life of comfort they had always known in the past couple of months have been stripped away.

Every individual loves the idea of the known. We like our comfort zones. We like our safe spaces. We get along with people who give us reason to be ourselves. We thrive in our communities and neighborhoods because we know everyone, and they know us.

We like our jobs because we have spent years at that same place, and we have become familiar. We have a relationship that is stable and at the slightest hint of it going wrong we begin to feel agitated.

Everyone craves stability. Humans are hardwired for it. But this has also created lots of room for anxiety, fear and the need to conform, even when things are not working out as we thought it should.

Charles Darwin once said: "it's not the specie that is smartest that survives but the one that is most adaptable to change."

As humans we have the capacity to adapt. To change and become better versions of ourselves. We are living in an age of constant change, where technological advancement has made it possible to witness new models of thinking and faster ways of getting things done.

As children one of the things, we quickly learn about life is that there are stages. We begin to learn how to crawl, then we walk, and then we sprint. We learn the alphabet then we learn small words and we move on to sentences. We move from toddlers to adolescents and then adults. From primary to tertiary institutions. We are constantly moving into the unknown. The only thing about the things mentioned is that we have been sort of programmed to expect them, so we are less perplexed at that reality. But everyone has his own journey into the unknown, even in the midst of these predictable patterns. That's why we see people struggle differently to fit into these different stages.

The key thing is to understand that to grow as an individual you must accept the reality of change. We must face the fact that we can't always figure out the trajectory of our life even when you have the blueprint. Within a drop of a dine something can alter the blueprint you created and that can be known and the unknown. Don't be afraid it will happen often, and you will be able to get better at handling the unknown.

The question then is How do we navigate the unknown? What do we do to bring ourselves to the place where we are able to constantly move into the unknown with the boldness that is required to conquer unfamiliarity? That is still apart of my journey.

The first thing is to assess the situation at hand. While it is good to have an optimistic view about life, it is also necessary to have a sense of what the situation entails. While the unfamiliar might seem unsettling. It is also relevant to look deeply into the situation and examine it critically. We could then realize that we have been exaggerating our fears after all. Assessment gives us a certain level of confidence.

One of my biggest issues is not being in control. But for me to gain control I have to be placed in an uncomfortable place. Here are a few examples. Have you ever been told by someone they need to have a talk with you? And if you ask about what they say I will let you know when we talk. Now depending on who it is you wonder what it could be, why couldn't they just say it right then and there. Frustration starts to build up and you begin to create scenarios in your head. This is because you have no control of the topic, but you are a part of the story. The unknown has now placed you in a bad place. However, once you hear the topic and you can relate or defend yourself you begin to be at ease.

We can't trust our impulse to make decisions because we may make decisions out of fear, anger, and lack of information. In assessing the situation, we can also look at the pros and cons of going into the unknown. How will it affect us in the long run?

Analyze and see what is at stake, is it worth it? Would it give you a better chance in life? Is it possible that you can speak with someone who has faced something similar? Are you sure you are not doing this for someone else? Is there something spurring you towards it? What are the possible dangers ahead?

Your assessment makes it possible for you to plan. When you have been able to weigh the consequences of your decisions it's then easy to know how to plan towards the execution. A lot of times people get overladen with fear of the unknown. They give up and turn their backs to advancing forward because they believe that to go into the unknown could strip them of their identities. But what if all you have been all your life, is leading you to that moment. What if you had to go through those situations just so you could become the best version of yourself? That's the point of analyzing the situation, it gives you a sense of your own capacities and what is required to move into the unknown.

Some unknown things are inevitable, like sudden death, the lost of a job, car accidents, unplanned pregnancies the list can go on and on. How we navigate through those unknown things in life is through experience, trial and error, and what I would say grace.

Your plans always reveal the state of your knowledge. Before plunging into the unknown have a firm view of your expectations. It would help in guiding you towards the relevant paths that you are to take note of.

When you know what you want out of life, it's easier to define yourself through the unfamiliar. You are not convicted by the uncertainties that lie ahead, rather, you are driven by the desire to accomplish what you have set your heart to do. And what matters in this situation is that you have already assessed what you may expect throughout the course of your journey.

Proper planning may not always get you all the answers, but rest assure that it will get you prepared in ways that would enable your advancement into the unknown more bearable.

There is also a place of caution. Most times when people find themselves in an unknown situation, they tend to be desperate for support. We must be careful of those who are not going the same way as us. They cannot give you the kind of support that is required, rather they may even persuade you from moving ahead because humans are programmed to crave after the predictable.

What do you think you can do to improve yourself to be better equipped in your journey when faced with the unknown? Can you look out for those who are also on that same path even though it's not the same? There is always someone who can offer some advice and even at that, you must be willing to be sure that you know what you are doing. I've used my own experience in the first chapter about someone who gave us wrong financial advice and how if we had done a thorough checkup, we would have been able to avoid the pitfall.

Be willing to get your hands dirty. What you desire and seek to become will never come on a platter. While your struggle is unique to you also realize that your predecessors were faced with the same uncertainties of life but were able to create a meaningful world for us in ways that we can find our own bearing. That's the beauty of embracing the unknown, you do not know what mark you are leaving behind in history to make the world a more coherent place for generations to come. Face the unknown with courage and faith knowing you can conquer anything and what doesn't kill you should make you stronger.

CHAPTER FOUR

STRATEGIES FOR OVERCOMING

How do we overcome situations? We first must go through it, face it, challenge it, be defeated and then defeat it. Strategies can be complexed when you didn't plan for it, but once you overcome it you begin to list that strategy for another situation and then it becomes more and more easier to strategize through life unexpected situations and challenges. Overcoming doesn't mean beating it just means you are ahead of it now. My biggest thought to myself is I can't fight the same thing twice I have to fight something new to have overcome the old. Let me give an example I use to be afraid of flying. I knew for me to see some of the world I needed to fly. I decided to get on the plane and sit near the window and look outside while the plane was taking off. I made up in my mind I was going to face my fear head on. And my longest flight has been to Africa.

When the world was hit with COVID, there was a lot of stressors as people lost their jobs, most had to stay at home, whole cities had to be lockdown and we soon realize that people were plunged in a state of despair because in the blink of an eye the life they had once understood was gone. As civilization advanced, we have begun to seek for easier ways to deal with situations and this has created a generation that struggles with adversity. We live in a world where we can tune off ourselves from dissenting views and recoil into our echo chambers not wanting to be faced with anyone with a contrary opinion.

We hammer on self-love and draw up criteria in which to relate with people. And we begin to see that over time we have created a system where we barely tolerate others. Our resilience is dwindling, and we are seeking easier and non-confrontational ways to navigate life. What we fail to realize is that life comes with the crooked and the straight. We must be willing to go through the discomfort at times to be able to have a more meaningful and richer life.

Uncertainties are a reality of life. One day you can have it all figured out and the next day you are grasping at what life has thrown at you. Instead of moaning about our loss and harping on what has been lost we can always look ahead and tell ourselves that if we have our breath then we can make the most of what life has thrown to us. My favorite motto is if I wake up the next day I have a second chance at it. We all have more second chances than we do first think about it. How do we turn these challenges into a strategy overcome them and make them opportunities?

Most of the things we overcome in life revolve around people. Humans are built for social interactions; we are not meant to live in isolation. How can we include strategies of overcoming life endeavors without including people. Studies have shown countless times that those who have a more robust connection with others tend to have a richer and more rewarding life. Less risk of heart related issues and a higher life expectancy. Covid almost isolated most of the population causing them to live in a world without others aside of from immediate family.

Think about someone who is struggling with an addiction, let's say alcoholism. Such people are always advised to join the alcoholic anonymous group. And we tend to see that such groups where people network and can share their struggles gives everyone else a sense that they are not battling with that addiction alone and they can always reach out when they need help.

Networking with others when you are faced with a situation helps you to get a perspective of things that are not just about you. You can begin to see how you can add the experience and knowledge of others in tackling that challenge. When you need help the best thing to offer yourself is the privilege of reaching out.

Another way of overcoming uncertainties and challenging situations is to face them and analyze worse case and best-case scenarios. What can you do differently from others? What are your potentials and talents and how well have you been able to harness them into something productive. It is often said that when life throws lemons at you, make lemonade. A lot of times we are more concerned about escaping our predicaments than making something out of that predicament. When you make it a duty to create things you soon find that your uniqueness plays out and makes you stand out.

Whatever you do be committed to seeing the world as a better place and while at it you will suddenly realize that there are the worst situations in the world.

Some of the most difficult experiences we encountered can serve as a source of inspiration to someone else. Most of the things we have learnt during our journey can go a long way in serving as a lesson to others. We often waste experiences because we do not see the lessons that are involved in it and when we are faced with challenges, we tend to see that it is always possible to repeat certain cycles because we have not been able to face our challenges enough to know and understand what we are capable of.

We tend to ignore the patterns that led us down those situations and see how they reoccur in subtle ways.

Learning the power of negotiations is a strategy of overcoming situations. Sometimes we have to negotiate in order to make a better situation, We often feel like we are out of options when faced with certain situations. It feels like we are being shortchanged and it makes us feel defeated. We sell ourselves short and look down on ourselves. We tell ourselves that we can't amount to much and this makes us reduce our own worth. We devalue ourselves and any opportunity that comes seems like a good one even when we are being taken advantage of.

When Sylvester Stallone had his big break with the Rocky franchise, he was homeless, he had sold his dog and the only thing he had was his dream of becoming an actor. He had his script written and when the time to negotiate came through, he decided that he was going to star in the movie as that was the only condition to release the script for production. Eventually the producers had no choice than to give in to his demands and today he is one of the most successful actors of his time. That's the power of negotiation. He negotiated his way out of his predicament. Also understand that your current situation does not in any way diminish your value. Yes, you are strategizing your life, embracing your power of overcoming obstacles that will soon make you greater and better than before.

Understand also that in the journey of life it is important to prioritize your challenges. Most times we may be struggling to keep up with sudden wealth or opportunities when we have not learnt how to build character to sustain those opportunities. It's the reason why most people who win lotteries and jackpots go broke after winning huge amounts. This is because they require knowledge that is needed to grow into what they have become, and it is not there.

While chasing success build character. Remember you are on a journey you're creating your own path for someone to follow. While seeking growth, strategies, challenges opportunities remember you will need to learn sacrifice. There are certain personal challenges we must overcome first.

Which means that challenges do not only have to do with external forces but also internal forces. How we self-sabotage relationships and opportunities. How we overlook what we are supposed to do. How we take certain things for granted. What you seem to admire in a person may have cost them a lot of sacrifices, challenged their souls, and be the last of all they had at the time. They are embracing their overcoming.

In overcoming challenges, we must understand that our priorities come first. We must never sacrifice the opportunity we have towards growth at the expense of sentiments. It's okay to leave certain people behind. It's okay to let go of what is holding you back. You cannot move ahead when you keep holding on to certain baggage. If it's meant to come it will catch up or just stay behind, it just maybe be time for new luggage.

A lot of circles should be limited. A lot of places hinder us from becoming the true version of ourselves. We may not realize it, but we have to understand that it is always important to see what we stand to gain as we strive to overcome the challenges. It is important to understand that you can't take everyone along on that journey.

You want to quit that addiction? Cut off from friends and places that reinforce it. You want to take up that business? Then put in the time to understudy it. Whatever it is you want to do always ensure that you selectively engage your energy towards it. It's pointless trying to crave for change and growth when you keep looking back at what's behind.

Another way to overcome challenges is to check your words and your thoughts. You can't give what you do not have. You cannot attract what you are not. And you certainly cannot become what you have not aspired towards.

Most people do not realize that they defeat themselves with their low self-esteem. They walk around with their heads hunched down. Their mind barren and lack of hope. They keep reinforcing the lie that they are not good enough. Can't do enough. Can't become anything more than they are. And when the opportunity presents itself, they fizzle away. Now your worth or spend time figuring it out then wanting more.

Here's the deal, you must treat yourself like you matter. You must always remind yourself that you have a value and a worth in creation. When you wake up every day remind yourself that you can make it and become someone useful in life. Whatever it is you are going through there is, a purpose. And that's the truth. Whatever we experience in life always has a way of defining us. If we choose to get bitter, we may never be able to set ourselves up as perfect examples of resilience. And we may go about hurting others because we feel hurt. Hurt people hurt people is the saying.

You are what you make of life. As hard as that sounds you have to understand that whatever challenges you have encountered on your journey, there are others like you who have risen from the situation to become better versions of themselves and to serve as inspiration to many people. That's the point, seeing your experience as a gift and making the most of it.

Without challenges there cannot be growth. In fact, we may never be able to know what we can become if we are not faced with adversity. That's why we have exams in schools to be tested of all the knowledge we have been given. That's life, it wants to know if you have been able to learn. It demands to be felt. To be made sense of. And the only way lessons can find some meaning is when you take little bits of your life and see the challenges inherent and decide to make it better. I have made my hardest lessons my biggest success. Dropping out of high school was the most challenging thing I went through. The disappointment of my family, the hardships of not having a high school diploma, the setbacks, and so much more. And now becoming an entrepreneur, an author, a motivational speaker, with two degrees. I made my biggest challenges my stepping stone to rise above and beat the odds of a high school dropout.

What you tell yourself matters a lot. You are a creature of growth. You are a creature of purpose. Your journey is unique, and you will become the best version of yourself. Remind yourself that it's only temporary. Believe it is important. What do you believe about yourself? Do you allow others define you?

Do you like truth? When we ask a lot of people these questions, they will tell you that they are all for the truth and they expect others to deal with them truthfully but as you get closer to them you see that accepting the truth about themselves is hard. When I accepted my truth and some of what people said about me to be true, I made some immediate changes. Not for others but for myself. The places I am going in life I must be able to take criticism and change it into a positive outlook that will further my future.

There are certain challenges that require us to accept the truth about ourselves. We must face the demons that we have created or the monsters that keep hindering us from becoming the best version of ourselves. We must look in the mirror and tell ourselves that if we intend to make things right then we must know that it begins with us.

This will require us going into areas that would make us uncomfortable. It will require us confronting certain realities about ourselves. It will require us to ask questions with answers that may not be pleasing to our ears. We must be truthful to ourselves, our ambitions and limitations, we must be truthful to our growth and our capacities. We must be truthful to our associations and our sacrifices. We must be truthful to our values and our priorities. This is the only way we can make the most of life. This is the only way we can try as much as we can to become relevant. This is the only way we can weed out those personal obstacles that we create on our path to discovery. And allow the seed to grow abundantly.

Another strategy is to acquire knowledge. A lot of times people plunge into situations and things without taking time to study the situation. We always feel like we have the capacity to do the things others have done and when we are faced with the same challenges, we are uncertain what to do. This is because everyone's obstacle is different and so is the outcome. Some people use their situation to be greater and some use it to feel sorrow and look for pittie.

Seek knowledge. Swallow your pride. Know all there is to know about your current challenges and be open to being taught. You cannot always be right. See yourself as a student in the school of life. Be willing to learn all there is to learn. Don't fake it because somehow. Allow yourself to go through the crushing of the grapes knowing you will become fine wine. When push comes to shove you will be your own investment to your destiny. It is not a waste. Invest in you, allow yourself the privilege of knowing what you don't know.

Also, learn to collaborate. As difficult as it may seem for people who are set in their own ways, one of the ways to make things easier is by collaborating with others who are doing something similar. Reach out to them and see how you can be beneficial to yourselves. I sat in rooms I thought I didn't belong in and eventual the rooms became mines. There are certain privileges that come as result of collaborations. You gain a richer perspective of life, and you become more exposed to the realities of your challenges. Avoid the need for isolation. Isolation is good after you have collaborated so you are able to identify what is needed in your life and the life's of those around you.

While it is true that not everyone is wired to mingle and while it is also true that certain situations warrant us keeping to ourselves. We also have modern tools that help us connect with the world. You can also create a new experience with people from other places and this can enable you to see your challenge in a new light. While I was in Africa I connected with new people and found new callings by just sharing my story. Isolation robs you of options. It creates a single narrative that is difficult to breakthrough from because you have made it your identity. And that challenge becomes amplified.

Here's a thing to also do, take note of patterns. Look at the frequency of the occurrence of your challenges and watch where you may have slipped.

There is always a pattern to things and often we do not easily see those patterns because we think things happen randomly. Certainly not.

Another important strategy is to know your strengths and weakness. What can you do better than everyone else? This could be your leverage. What do you have to offer the world? What knowledge do you think may be beneficial for the advancement of humanity? Do you have skill or will. Skill will get you a job Will can make you the owner of the business. Most times we live in obscurity because we feel we do not have anything to offer the world. We are so far from the truth. When you have mastered your strength, you have an edge over your challenges because you are able to apply that knowledge in overcoming the situation and it makes it easy to know what you outsource.

Your weaknesses help you to keep you in check. It helps you not to get complacent. Your weakness helps you to stay on your toes. You don't get carried away because you understand that there's power in your armor. You are guarded and able to take conscious steps into ensuring that you become better at managing your weakness because it often turns out that our weaknesses have a way of compounding our challenges when we fail to put them in check. Make your weakness your strength at some point.

A lot of things can be avoided when we know ourselves. A lot of situations are self-inflicted and for those that are not there's always a way that we can complicate issues for ourselves if we fail to understand how to handle what has failed us.

Most people seek the easy way out, but we must understand that a life that must overcome challenges must face whatever is coming ahead.

A wise man once said, the price for freedom is eternal vigilance.

CHAPTER FIVE

LOOKING AHEAD

What do you see? A lot of times our perception affects our reality. Going to the moon would not have been possible if those someone didn't look ahead and think it could happen. First, they saw the moon as a place that could be reached. Then the technology to make it happen became necessary. When people say necessity is the mother of all inventions what they simply mean is that what we see determines what we create. I know look forward to what is ahead so I can plan for it. Even if my plans do not play out, I am still looking ahead because I know one day it will. Once you have hope anything is possible in this world according to my husband.

If you want to build a house, you first draw out the design and have a plan on how you want it to go. You have a structure that is defined and followed according to the details of the architect. There's nothing that we see around us that was not first conceived in the mind. Even though life has gone away of changing our plans, like we get up with the intensions of running outside, but we woke up with a pain in our leg so instead we must walk. The key is continuing to work towards what is ahead.

What you feed your mind with determines what you see. To see far, you must understand that our capacity for conception is infinite, and the only limitations are the ones we set for ourselves. If we say we can't then we won't.

Life will give us according to the measure of what we believe. Never underestimate the power of walking by faith because it has a way of pointing you towards what you can become even if you're uncertain.

What you think has a way of defining your priorities. Your thoughts mainly come from your feelings at the time. Most times we borrow the view of others. Maybe because it's more glamorous, maybe because we believe that the grass is greener on that side of their view. We then begin to find that the realities do not match. We have been living on another person's blueprint and we can no longer live up to this expectation anymore.

Your sight can determine your drive. It dictates your direction. Your sight can show you what you must do to get to where you want to be. Without our sight we can always lose track of where we are headed. Without our sight we can lose our way. Without our sight we can become clueless. That's the point. We must understand that sight is powerful. Without it you cannot bring anything into existence. Sight is more than visual it should be considered looking ahead even in the mind.

And when we talk about sight, we are referring to the eye of the mind. What the mind sees. You can only go as far as you see. Your sight represents your vision. It gives you a purpose. You can see it as a path that is being carved out by virtue of your perception. Anytime I am not feeling good, or something is going on my husband would say "this time next week you will feel better or it will be better" and it always eased my mind to know what I was feeling wouldn't last forever so I looked ahead mentally.

Too many people have no sight of who they are. They have no sight of what they are. They have no sight of how they intend to even get to their destinations. So, it becomes difficult to navigate the journey. There are ways in which you can develop your sight.

One of the ways to see clearly is to watch the things you gravitate towards. What are those things that easily come to you? Your sight has a way of revealing itself in your desires. But you need to articulate your thoughts clearly to see what you have concealed inside of you.

In the journey of life, the only way to look ahead is to have vision.

What do you seek? Now that you have been able to define what you see you then begin to narrow it down. What's your own path in the journey? The finished line for a hundred meter's race is not the same for someone running a marathon. What you seek keeps your focus steady. A lot of times people talk about moving on but find that they are stuck in their mind.

They do not know what they are seeking. It's only an emotion depending on how they are feeling at the time.

Most people get what they think they want out of life and soon realize that an emptiness tugs at their heart. It's as if all they had labored to get had been nothing but a waste of time, but time is only wasted when you don't make nothing of the time that has gone. If you don't do anything with the time that was wasted, you can start to self-destruct.

Learn to count on past experiences. This gives you the sense of your progression. So, when situations arise that are similar you can draw from the wealth of past knowledge into tackling the current situation. It has the tendency to resurface in the future. And it could come as a baggage that weighs you down on your journey ahead. Pay attention to the lessons of the past while you look ahead.

So, you have seen. You have sought. You have counted on past experiences to grow some knowledge. It's time to carve a path for yourself. You have a unique set of qualities peculiar to you alone. Your path is what defines your journey, and you can build your road ahead.

You cannot run in someone else's lane when in a race. You either get disqualified or cause an accident. A lot of people are walking about today treading a path meant for someone else and it becomes too late to even understand where they are headed anymore. It's only when you have a clearly defined path that you can look towards where the journey is headed. Going in a wrong direction sets you back during your journey. Have a clearly defined path and walk in it. How do you create that path you learn from mistakes and use your mistakes as a steppingstone to move up.

Beware of side attractions. There is a saying that says if you stop to throw a stone at every dog that barks at you, you will never get to your destination. In moving forward there are certain things that we do not need to carry along with us. We may feel like we need them on the journey, but we soon realize that they weigh us down and limit our speed. Hurt and pain is one of them. If we stop to grieve, we will be at that place for a long time. Remember you don't get over grief, you learn how to live with it.

A lot of times we do not want to hurt people. So, we try to compromise to give room for them. Know who is worth tagging along and who isn't. Note those who are relevant to the course of your journey and those who are merely passing by. Both people play apart in your life and is apart of your journey.

I see people trying to carry everyone along with them. While this is noble, you must understand that you can't carry everyone along. Not everyone sees what you see. History is filled with men who were mocked for their beliefs and their ambitions before it became a reality. I have tried to carry people along with me, because I didn't want to hear I changed. The reality is I cannot be the same, every day is different; life is changing, and I am learning new and better ways of handling myself and others. Therefore, change is relevant to everyone's journey.

It is dangerous to go on a journey with someone who doesn't see the same thing that you see. My husband and I are very different but share the same values, we want the same things in life such as, the ability to care for our parents, a comfortable affordable lifestyle, good health, our children to be ambitious. We both see the future as our life experience. Although this is a marriage the same values can be in social, business, and other relationships. rid

As we move ahead in life, we begin to realize some of the things that we held on to were pointless because they are gone, we are the ones holding on to them. Some of our past things we allow to define us, may hinder us. There is nothing wrong with remembering the past but trying to live in it is a different thing. Keep what helps you grow, get rid of what stunts your growth.

In fact, there's is always a high tendency that when you fail to let go you limit yourself from getting something better. Do not be afraid to let go of the past, just make it available so you know where you don't ever want to be again.

Whenever you are tempted to give up remind yourself why you started in the first place. Whenever it gets so weary and you do not feel like doing it anymore ask yourself what you would rather be, a coward who was not able to finish what was started or a champion whose testimony would serve as an inspiration for others.

Looking ahead means seeing the obvious obstacles and still choosing to move ahead regardless. There is so much to explore in life including our trials. The things that hurt you may save someone else, and there will be your reward, your testimony, your victory, your why me.

CHAPTER SIX

CONTINUING THE JOURNEY

What makes a journey interesting is the capacity to anticipate what lies ahead. Expectation has a way of making us agile in our pursuit through life. We have a sense that we are moving towards something until life ends. We must always recreate our focus as we move closer to our destination. Look at your life in different directions. Look at your journey in different directions. Do not seem content when you have reached a certain height, and by this I am not talking about greed that possess a person till they lose their senses and start to inflict pain on others. I am referring to the ability to continue to set up new aims as you have ahead.

The journey can only get exciting when you do not act like you have seen it all. There's so much life has to offer and the best you can do is to ensure that you pick those things apart while on your journey. Examine it critically and ask yourself what that is there can still be done. How do I make the world a better place than I met it? These questions have a way of keeping us humble. It makes us realize that there's always more to be done. A life devoid of expectations sooner or later begins to whither and lose its vivacity.

To sustain our wonder about life we must seek more. Curiosity must be our best friend. We must always ask questions. We must always be willing to seek. To know. To learn, to explore, to be hurt and to heal. We must always be intentional about sustaining the delight of life and its encounters.

This can only come from having an open mind and planning for the best but preparing for the worst and overcoming the worse with the initial plans. Let me further explain. Most times when something bad happens we get distracted and our plans for the day, week, month and year has to change. The issue is people forget to go back to the initial plan once they figure out what went wrong. They begin to create new plans and then are faced with not accomplishing things. Get back on track. The journey still needs to go on, the plans still should remain and become even better because you have now learned how to navigate through a distraction. Every day we see new discoveries, and this gives us a sense that is universe is inexhaustible.

We cannot fathom all there is to it if we keep a cynical look towards it. There must be a burning anticipation of what life has to offer. New places to see. New friends to make. New connections to link up with. New territories for expansion. Africa was a life experience that I will never forget. I sometimes think to myself and say "I would have never thought I would travel across the world". Those thoughts were because my circumstances at the time would never lead me to believe I would make it there.

Don't become too familiar with life that you fail to see that life is not just about aiming at a target but a process of constantly evolving and moving towards the target. You will get hit by darts and be able to bring thing with you as a prize.

What are your goals at each level of your life? How do you know what kind of goals to set? These are questions that we are often plagued with in our journey through life. And sometimes don't have an answer until something happens that wakes us up and we are forced to set goals, like having children, falling in love, wanting a house, a car, clothes, shoes, the essential things in life. I would say adult time.

Here is a thing to consider. We must move in the direction of the goals that we set for us to be able to make a meaning out of life. When we fail to set goals, we are like a rudderless ship without direction. Sooner or later, we will realize that we have not been able to make any sense of how our life is headed. Goals help us to see what we are up against in the journey of life. Goals help us to become more attuned with the reality of our current state and what we aspire towards. Goals can be changed; however, you should still want the goal to hold value. You should set your goal and try to keep it to show your capability of keeping your word to yourself. I set goals and try to keep them, because I can't get mad if others let me down and I let my own self down. We teach people how to treat us according to how we treat ourselves.

When we set goals, it gives us something to look forward to. Most of the time we must come to terms with the fact of the reality of setting goals. We cannot amount to much in our journey through life if we do not know where we are headed and what we desire out of life. Goals help us to create a perception of what we want. You can also say goals are a way of seeking out the meaning of our journey. Some of us have had an exciting journey that we have been on this far. Have you ever thought about sharing your journey with someone? Or the world? The thoughts are who will listen. My answer is the people who need to hear it. My first book was my personal journal, my past, my pain, my accomplishments who better to tell your story than you. You do not know whose life you may help by sharing your story of what you have overcome and what is in your future.

What we aim to improve, and what we intend to leave behind should be legacies built from goals and ambition. We must be sure that we have the resources to achieve them and when we see that we do not have them we have to be willing to seek out the relevant means in which we can attain these goals. Most of your resources are your trials, the things that didn't work for you. Being able to accept where you went wrong and what you could have done differently can go a long way. Resources are not always money. Resources are things accessible to you, you may need to research it or you may just stumble across them. The key is how you use it.

Note that any goal that is self-serving cannot give any long-lasting fulfillment. Your goal in the journey of life should be able to make the world a better place for you and someone else. You may not be able to rescue everyone, but you can certainly do your best to make sure that your goal is able to inspire others.

Clarify your goals for each stage of your life. Understand what you are aiming for and what you are living for. Know that the peculiarity of your goal is depended on the path you have been set on. Ensure that you have goals that outlive you, goals that others coming behind can latch on to.

How well do you understand your process in this journey? Most times people get frustrated when things are not going as planned, which is natural.

Most times we find ourselves in situations where we have tried all that we know and nothing seems to work out, it makes us overwhelmed. This just means it's time to find another way to do it.

We can't seem to understand why there is a stop in our progress. We are trying to forge ahead but it seems we are stuck. We want to do something different, but don't know what. That is the time to step back and analyze the goal, see if it's realistic, does it have a value to your life and your journey.

What happens in this is, we are learning resilience. We are learning to build our capacity to be creative in situations. We do not often see this because we are at that point where we believe that everything should fall in place for us. It could also be a serious period of regret. Remember the saying "anything worth having is worth work for".

We may feel that we have lost opportunities. We may feel that we have lost privileges. We may feel that we are not where we are supposed to be. We begin to think of all sorts of things that make us question if we are on the right path. We are on the right path, obstacles are made to be gone through. Do not question the path, figure it out.

Here's the deal, have you sat down to ask yourself if there is more to what you are going through? Have you ever thought about the fact that you are where you are because you are learning something that is meaningful to your journey?

Understand your process and learn all there is for that stage of your life. It could be that you are not paying attention to something that requires your attention, it could be that you are getting complacent. It could just be that you need to see things differently.

Whatever you are faced with, always take note of the fact that you are going through a process. Certain plants germinate annually, others biennially while there are some that germinate perennially. They all have their seasons and their purposes.

When in your season understand the need for gratitude. Gratitude for where you are coming from. Gratitude for how far you have been able to move ahead in your journey.

It's always relevant to be grateful because it gives you a fresh perspective about life. Without gratitude life can be frustrating and boring, without gratitude life can become a chore and it can make you feel like you are just waltzing through. But when you are grateful you can navigate your process with ease. Just be grateful you woke up that is always a start.

Run from comparison. This cannot be overemphasized. In the age of social media and the need for a picture-perfect life. We have gradually lost the value of appreciating the little things of life. What we find most of the times is that we compare our lives with the perfect view that people portray, and we fail to see that they only show us the beautiful parts of their lives. They do not show us their struggles and pain. Their discontent. The uncertainties that lurk in the corners of their heart. I want you to see it all, so when you see me happy you say she deserves to be happy.

We are carried away by the glitz and glamour and we are blindsided by envy. We do not see what we are doing to ourselves. The damage of comparison is that it robs us of contentment. We fail to see what we are meant to be instead we see ourselves through others. I lived that way for years and once I stepped away, I found my own path and was able to navigate through my journey.

As we journey through life, we must understand that everyone is facing their own struggles, and no one has it all figured out.

Most people cry behind the camera and try as much as they can to conceal it from the world. Avoid seeing your life from another person's experience. You have a whole life ahead of you and trying to be like everyone and anyone robs you of your authenticity.

Does it mean we should not emulate those who have gone ahead of us? Far from that. There are lots of things to learn from people who have gone ahead of us. But the danger of comparison is that you are not learning, you are competing. You are assessing your life if it measures up to the standard of someone else. You are depriving yourself of growing at your own pace.

You are becoming agitated and scared. You are petrified at every turn. You are beginning to see things from the life of someone else. You lose your essence and your identity. You lose your purpose.

There are certain things about life that you must understand about yourself and one of them is that you are not everyone else. You cannot be tied to the identity of others neither should you be defined by the label of others. What counts as success to a doctor would not be the same for a rock star.

What counts as a challenge for the priest would not be the same for an astronaut. Everyone has a unique set of abilities and capacities required for each stage of their life. On my journey I hope to help others find what's needed to be self-fulfilled to be their authentic self, so they are able to continue on their journey and utilize every lesson.

The danger of comparison is that you deprive yourself of knowing what you can become. You deprive the world of your awesomeness. You lose track of your journey. You forfeit what defines you. You soon realize that you are subjected to the whim of others.

You should be able to accept the fact that where you are is just a temporary experience and there is more to you where you are headed. It's the lack of patience that births frustration. Wait your turn. My husband and I waited our turn, to buy a car, to buy a home, to travel, to do a little more for our kids. We cheered on others and waited our turn. God knew when it was our time do the things we wanted but during that tine we took the necessary steps in our journey to move towards the things that we wanted. What is for you, you will have.

Why would you want to become someone else when they cannot even be you? Your fingerprint is unique. That says a lot about why you are called for a different purpose. You do not want to get to someone else's destination and soon realize that you have been living a life that is not yours. That is a recipe for crisis.

Be at peace with your stage of the journey. Let your goals be what motivates you. Do not be content with mediocrity. Mediocrity is always a response to fear. Mediocrity can be a result of not being confident enough in yourself. So, you do the bare minimum to get by. How unfair is that to your self aren't you worth more than the bare minimum.

Have you noticed that the world does not celebrate mediocrity? Because we realize that for you to have been able to rise above others in your endeavors, you must have put in the effort that is required into achieving that feat. The problem with mediocrity is that it is a great disservice to all that you have been given to journey through life.

Be willing to pay the price. You can easily tell how well a person believes in themselves by how hard they strive for their achievements.

What are you willing to do during your journey to get towards the goals you have set out? Talk is cheap. Ideas on paper are just ideas. Even if you write them on a digital gadget, they are just words on screen and until you implement them, they have no effect.

That means for everything we aim towards we should also count the cost. What does it mean for us and how much are we willing to give to what it takes?

Lots of people get carried away by trends, they do not have an identity of their own. They are a product of the system. Their opinions are not theirs. Their lives are not theirs. They just move through life consuming everything that is thrown at them. Their lives are vacuous. Void of substance.

To continue this journey of life there must be a certain level of peace that comes from a place of contentment with who you are ordained to be.

There is so much that you must live for beyond materialism beyond the constant crave to fit in. Most times we do not even know what we want on this journey but all along we have always been given a voice inside of us nudging us towards the inevitable. We have always been that person, but we have not really known it all along because our inner voice is always silenced by the expectations of others. Our journey is a constant process of self-discovery.

You must let go of past disappointments. Reminiscing on the past can only stunt your growth. Past failures are not a prerequisite to determine current endeavors. Instead, we should always see that whatever must have transpired in the past is best left in the past. Holding on to pain, guilt, and the bad energies of the past will only hinder us from maximizing the best of the opportunities we have going forward. The past is a lesson. Learn from it and move forward in your journey. I am still learning that my past doesn't determine my future, it helps shift things around and teaches me growth, empowerment, lessons, good and bad. I am not proud of all my decisions in life, but I am happy I took something from them and made a change for the best. I wouldn't encourage a teenage ro drop out of high school and obtain a GED, but I would show them someone who obtained a GED and is successful and never gave up.

I had the opportunity to speak at a school for teenage girls who were pregnant or have already become mothers from the ages of 12years old to 18 years old. I looked into eye of my self-31 years ago and saw fear of the unknown. When I sat in a seat like them all I had was thoughts that I failed, and I was a disappointment to my family. I spoke from that place and spoke to my younger self saying the things I would have wanted to hear. "Life isn't over" "You can still be who you want" "this is a minor set back for a bigger come up". You see remembering what you been through isn't always bad if you use it to influence someone else.

A lot of times we move on and we forget about those who are coming behind us. There's an African proverb that says the horse in front always looks at the one behind when running. This means that we have been saddled with the responsibility of ensuring that as we move ahead in life, we help others who are coming along to define themselves through the paths that we have created.

It means we cannot afford to live a carefree life as we have been given the opportunity to become a beacon of hope to generations. If you fail to take up the responsibility you will soon realize that all of your life you have been living for yourself without testing the veracity of your discoveries. Those who come behind can always help you to see the flaws in your journey and improve on it. Especially your kids. You ever wander why parents say do as I say not as I do.

We are often scared of being demystified, especially when we have become an authority in our journey. The point is, create a path that others can follow. It gives you a sense that you have been able to leave a legacy. But don't be drunk by it. Being able to fix mistakes if not it's the fastest way to a downfall.

To recreate ourselves we must be able to give ourselves the privilege of finding out new ways of discovering life. We must be constantly open to growth and the changing of times. We must see that life is not about what we know but what we need to know.

I look at how far I have come along my journey. And I see that without fortitude one may never amount to much. I see that the journey is never ending, and the destination is always in the future. It doesn't matter what we acquire. It does not matter what we become. It does not matter where we go, we are always going to be on a journey, physically, mentally and spiritually.

Experiencing certain aspects of life is a solo experience but never a solo trip. To continue this journey, we need people who share the same values that we share so that when we get to situations when it feels like we can no longer do it on our own we have a community to fall back to. We need people who will be there when push comes to shove, this means that we must be specific about our affiliations. Do that mean dismiss people or take them out of your life? Of course not, however you must pick and choose who you know verses who you entertain.

To make the most of this journey always have a journal. If you need to reminisce on the past by looking back on how far you have come. Just don't dwell on it, remember it is gone. It can help you to articulate your thoughts. It helps to point you in the direction you are meant to go.

As we move forward, we must be willing to see that what lies ahead is more important than what is behind us.

CONCLUSION

If you have been able to take walk with me till the end of this book, I hope you were able to get the gist of my continued journey. Which included trials and tribulations, disappointments, ups, downs, lessons, findings, information, advice, circumstances encouragements and whatever you were able to take from it to help you along the way.

My goal in this book is to take the reader through my continued journey and give real life examples along with ideas on how to create a path for a successful journey. I provided life experience and personal thoughts on what I thought helped me and what hurt me. My goal is to also share my story. In my first book I stated that I want to be able to tell my own story.

I hope that at every point in your walk you can see that it is not the speed that counts but the accuracy of the journey.

You do not have to have it all figured out. Trust me, there is no one on earth who has it all figured out.

I hope during your journey you can learn to forgive yourself if you have any mistakes of the past and to give yourself the privilege of trying again.

I hope that you see yourself as a process and not as finished work. Take yourself away from the pressure of expectations.

I hope you learn that when life happens at an unexpected time, it is not because you failed at something, it can be just to call your attention to how vulnerable we can be as humans during our journey and to make you have a reference for what you have been able to become.

I hope that as you go through life you find what you really want, and you can see through the vanity of your own desires to crave for something lasting and tangible.

I want you to understand that you have the liberty of becoming anything you set your heart to if you are honest enough to challenge your limitations.

I hope you understand that through challenges the unfamiliar becomes familiar. Figure out what drives you and be great at it. Challenges build character. Take the Challenge and Conquer it! It's ok to be disliked for who you are than liked for who you are not!

I hope you use my journey as a guiding force to help you along the way. Try your best to live life to the fullest. Learn from every experience. CREATE YOUR PATH and continue your journey.

Sincerely,

Georgiana Smith CEO, MHA, BA, Author, Motivator, SURVIVOR